THE SUPER SCIENCE BOOK OF ENERGY

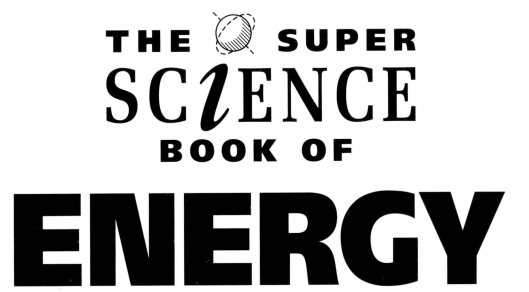

Jerry Wellington

Energy

Bright suns and silent nuns
Curled-up cats and hanging bats
Windmills and cash tills
Electric fires and rolling tires
The salty sea and bouncing me
We all have energy

Energy gets us going
Gets things flowing
Not a rustle
Or a muscle
Could we move
Or groove
Without energy

by Lizzie Lewis

Illustrations by Frances Lloyd

Thomson Learning
New York

Titles in the Super Science series

Energy
The Environment
Forces
Life Processes
Light
Materials

Our Bodies
Rocks and Soils
Sound
Space
Time
Weather

First published in the United States in 1994 by
Thomson Learning
115 Fifth Avenue
New York, NY 10003

First published in Great Britain in 1994 by
Wayland (Publishers) Ltd.

Library of Congress Cataloging-in-Publication Data
Wellington, J. J. (Jerry J.)
  The super science book of energy / Jerry Wellington;
illustrations by Frances Lloyd.
      p.   cm. – (Super science series)
  Includes bibliographic references and index.
  ISBN 1-56847-222-6
  1. Force and energy – Juvenile literature. 2. Power
resources – Juvenile literature. [1. Force and energy.
2. Power resources.] I. Lloyd, Frances, ill. II. Title.
III. Series: Super science.
QC73.4.W44   1994
333.79 – dc20   94-4210

Printed in Italy

Series Editor: Jim Kerr
Designer: Loraine Hayes Design

Picture Acknowledgments

Illustrations by Frances Lloyd
Cover illustration by Martin Gordon

Photographs

Action Plus 4 bottom; Chapel Studios 12 top (Jayne Knights);
Bruce Coleman 16 top (Fritz Prenzel); Eye Ubiquitous 6 (Tim
Page), 28 (Jim Holmes); Performing Arts Library 22 (Steve
Gillett); Science Photo Library 10 (Sheila Terry), 11 (Alex
Bartel), 12 bottom left (Martin Bond), 16 bottom (Martin
Bond), 17 (U.S. Department of Energy), 19 (Francoise Sauze),
25 (Peter Menzel); Tony Stone Worldwide 12 bottom right
(Robin Smith), 15 (Gerald Fritz), 18 (Glen Allison), 20 (Colin
Raw); Quadrant 4 top; Wayland Picture Library 8, 14, 27 top
left, 27 top right (Jimmy Holmes); ZEFA 24, 27 bottom
(R. Bond).

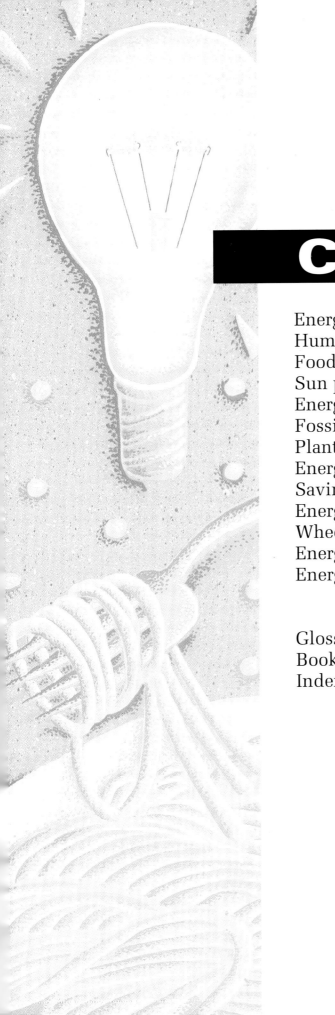

CONTENTS

ENERGY ALL AROUND

It's hard to say exactly what energy is, but we can say that there is energy all around us and we cannot live without it.

A moving racing car has energy. ▶ Running water in a mountain stream has energy. An Olympic sprinter running in a 100-meter race has energy. All of these things have energy because they are moving – so energy has something to do with movement. Sometimes the movement is not so obvious. For example, a person playing a musical instrument has energy and the sound produced by the instrument has energy.

But some things that are not moving have energy. The water held back by a huge dam has energy. If the dam burst you would clearly see this energy. A stretched rubber band has energy. Let it go and it snaps back. The sun has energy. Without solar energy, we would all die. The different fuels we use – gasoline, oil, and natural gas – all have energy. So you can see that energy comes in many different forms. They are all important, and human beings depend on them for their survival. Without energy there would be no life on earth.

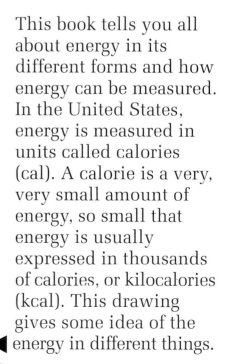

Energy in a sugar cube
25 kcal

Energy used
playing soccer for 60 minutes
500 kcal

Energy from burning
1 lb. of coal
3,500-3,800 kcal

Energy in
1 gallon of
gasoline
21,000-24,000 kcal

Electrical energy released
from a large power plant
in 1 second   5000,000 kcal

Energy released by
an H-bomb   2,000,000+ kcal

This book tells you all about energy in its different forms and how energy can be measured. In the United States, energy is measured in units called calories (cal). A calorie is a very, very small amount of energy, so small that energy is usually expressed in thousands of calories, or kilocalories (kcal). This drawing gives some idea of the energy in different things.

5

HUMAN ENERGY

All of us need energy to stay alive. Our bodies are made up of organs (such as the heart, stomach, liver, brain, and lungs). All of our organs need energy to work. Our hearts need energy to pump blood around the body. Our stomachs and other organs of our digestive systems need energy to digest food. Our nerves need energy to carry messages to and from the brain. Taking in fresh air and breathing out stale air also requires energy, so we use energy even when we sleep.

Young people who are still growing ▶ and women who are pregnant need extra energy. If we are working hard or exercising, we need extra energy. A marathon runner needs a lot of energy to run for twenty-six miles.

Human energy comes from food and drink. Long-distance runners often carry special high-energy drinks with them to replace the energy they use when running.

Person		Energy intake (kcal/day)	
Baby	800-1,000		
6-year-old	1,800	15- to 17-year-old male	3,100
		15- to-17-year-old female	2,200
18- to 34-year-old active male	2,800		
18- to 34-year-old active female	2,100		
Pregnant woman	2,400	75-year-old	1,800

◀ All human beings are different, though. A pregnant woman needs more than a young girl. This drawing shows the approximately how much energy is needed each day by different people.

Even though most of ▶ us aren't long-distance runners, we still need lots of energy to do everyday things. This drawing shows the energy that we use in one minute during different activities. Notice that while we are asleep, we use about one kilocalorie every minute.

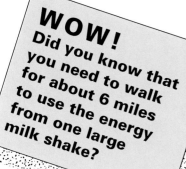

WOW!
Did you know that you need to walk for about 6 miles to use the energy from one large milk shake?

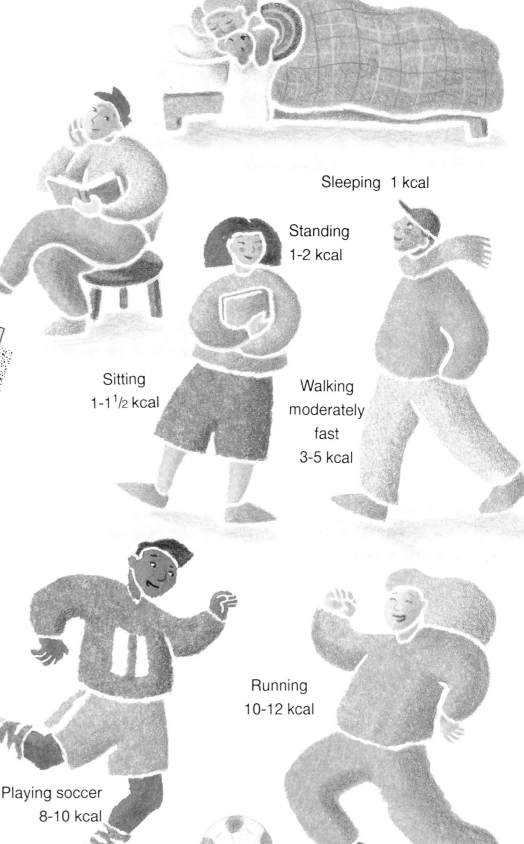

Sleeping 1 kcal

Standing
1-2 kcal

Sitting
1-1$\frac{1}{2}$ kcal

Walking
moderately
fast
3-5 kcal

Going upstairs
9-10 kcal

Running
10-12 kcal

Playing soccer
8-10 kcal

FOOD, GLORIOUS FOOD

If you look at the labels on packages or cans of food, you will see that the foods contain vitamins, proteins, carbohydrates, and fat. Vitamins and minerals help to keep various parts of our bodies healthy, such as our hair and teeth. Proteins help us to grow and maintain our bodies. A balanced diet must contain enough vitamins, minerals, and proteins, but it must also provide us with fuel – energy to keep us going. This comes mainly from foods containing sugar and starch, or carbohydrates. This photo shows some energy-giving food and drink. Sugary items give us short-term energy; items with complex carbohydrates (potatoes or cereal) are healthier energy-givers. ▶

When sugar or starch is digested, chemical products form. The blood carries these products to various cells in our bodies. Inside the cells, the products mix with oxygen (which the blood has brought from our lungs) and release energy.

cherry
2-3 kcal

carrot
20 kcal

apple
65 kcal

poached egg
70 kcal

bread and
butter
150 kcal

8 oz.
whole milk
160 kcal

1 cup cornflakes
with skim milk
180 kcal

fast food
burger
and fries
500-800 kcal

◀ Different foods contain different amounts of energy, which is usually measured in kilocalories (kcal), though on labels kilocalories are called calories. This drawing shows you the calories in some of the things you may eat and drink.

Look again at the labels on food ▶ packages. These will tell you how much energy is contained in the food. To enable us to compare the amount of energy in, say, cereal and chocolate, food labels usually state how many calories (really kilocalories) are contained in one serving of the food.

Whenever you eat or drink, you take in energy. As you have seen, you use energy when you are working or moving around, and your body needs energy in order to grow and stay warm. It is important that the energy you take in every day roughly balances the energy you use.

Daily energy needs

Look back at the drawing on page 6 showing how much energy people need in one day. Figure out breakfast, lunch, and dinner menus for one boy and one girl in your class at school. Try to find out how many kilocalories are contained in each meal.

Will the three meals supply them with enough energy for their daily needs?

WOW!
If you lift an apple from the floor up to a table about 3 feet high, you use one kilocalorie or less of energy. If you ate the same apple it would give you about 65 kilocalories of energy.

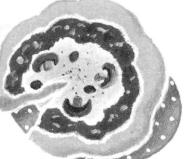

9

SUN POWER

The green leaves of plants trap energy from sunlight.

The sun is our nearest star. Nearly all of the energy that we use on earth comes from the sun. Millions of years ago it helped to form fossil fuels such as coal, oil, and natural gas. Now, it helps plants and trees to grow, and these provide us with energy.

All of the energy in the food we eat ▶ comes from plants. Plants store energy from the sun. When the sun's rays reach plants, the leaves use the rays to make sugar and starch. These are stored in the plants and will give us energy when we eat them. We eat some plants, such as lettuce and potatoes, directly, but we also eat plants indirectly when we eat meat from animals that have fed on plants.

◀ Enough energy from the sun falls on the earth every day to provide all of the energy that the human race needs for one year! The problem is that we need to collect and capture this energy. One way of doing this is to use solar panels. You may have seen solar panels on the roofs of some houses. The panels absorb some of the sun's energy. This energy can then be used to do things such as heat water. Obviously, solar panels work best in sunny places like Florida or Arizona, but they can still be used in cloudy places.

◀ Another way of collecting energy from the sun is to use a large solar furnace. These collect the sun's rays and use shiny mirrors to focus them on a small area. Some solar furnaces can heat to temperatures of up to 5,500°F.

WOW!
The temperature of the sun is about 10,000°F at its surface and over 25 million °F inside!

We can also store energy from the sun by converting it directly into electricity. Electricity produced by solar cells is used to power satellites, which are spacecraft that travel around the moon, the earth, or another planet and send back information to earth. ▼

Which surface is best for a solar panel?

Try using different surfaces, such as aluminum foil, shiny wrapping paper, ordinary white paper, dark paper of different colors, and black paper. Wrap same-sized pieces of each type of paper around similar-sized objects such as bricks or blocks of wood. Leave each object in the sun for about ten minutes, then feel which object is the warmest. What do you find?

ENERGY
THROUGH THE AGES

◀ People have used the sun as their main energy source ever since life on earth began. The sun indirectly provides us with energy from running water. Heat from the sun evaporates water from lakes and the sea. This falls again from the clouds as rain and runs downhill. Running water has been used for centuries to turn waterwheels and is now used to turn turbines.

Energy from the wind has been used for many centuries. Wind in the earth's atmosphere is the movement of air caused by the uneven heating of the earth's surface by the sun. These photos show an old windmill and a modern wind turbine. The wind turbine is used to generate electricity. The wind turns the blades of the wind turbine. As the blades go around, a large generator turns inside the wind turbine, which produces electricity. The windmill is used to turn a
▼ millstone.

Firewood is fuel that provided energy for cave dwellers thousands of years ago and is still used in many parts of the world for cooking and heating. It is a fuel used mainly in countries where people cannot afford to buy oil, gas, or coal to use in their homes.

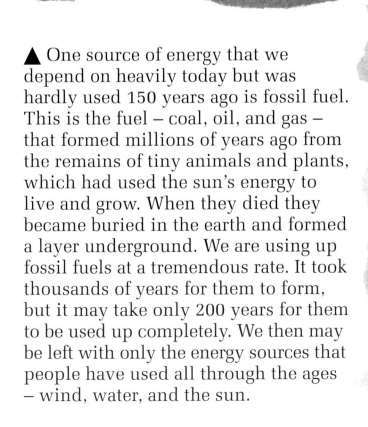

Millions of years ago, there were great forests.

These gradually decayed to form swamps. Over many years, new layers of rock formed, pressing down on the swamps.

Under this pressure, the swamps turned to coal, oil, and gas, which people now use for fuel.

▲ One source of energy that we depend on heavily today but was hardly used 150 years ago is fossil fuel. This is the fuel – coal, oil, and gas – that formed millions of years ago from the remains of tiny animals and plants, which had used the sun's energy to live and grow. When they died they became buried in the earth and formed a layer underground. We are using up fossil fuels at a tremendous rate. It took thousands of years for them to form, but it may take only 200 years for them to be used up completely. We then may be left with only the energy sources that people have used all through the ages – wind, water, and the sun.

FOSSIL FUELS

We live in the age of fossil fuels. ▶
This pie chart shows where the
world's energy comes from. You can
see that today it comes almost entirely
from the three fossil fuels.

The fossil fuels are all excellent
sources of energy. They can be
removed from beneath the earth's
surface by drilling into the ground.
The structure in the picture, an oil rig,
is used to remove oil from under the
sea. The energy from fossil fuels can be
released by burning them. Fossil fuel
energy is used in industry, for farming,
for transportation, and for heating
homes and offices. ▼

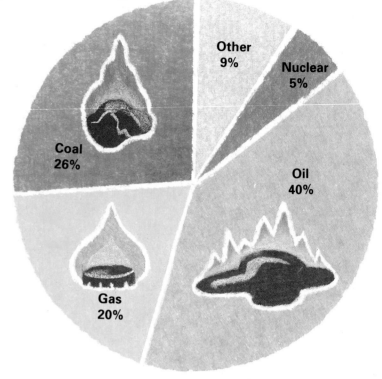

Other 9%

Nuclear 5%

Coal 26%

Oil 40%

Gas 20%

Although fossil fuels are excellent sources of energy, we are using them up and they can't be replaced. No one is sure exactly how long they will last, but some people believe that the world's oil may run dry in about fifty years from now. Gasoline for trucks and cars comes from oil. What will our vehicles run on when there is no oil left? We may run out of natural gas, too, in about fifty years. Then how will we heat our homes? The supply of coal is likely to last longer, maybe for 300 years, but it will not last forever.

Another problem ▶ with fossil fuels occurs when we burn them to release their energy. They all produce gases of one sort or another, such as the exhaust fumes from cars that run on gasoline. This photo shows the smog from car exhaust fumes hanging over New York City.

WOW!
There are more than 120 million cars in the U.S., and they use more than 25 percent of the world's gasoline.

PLANT POWER

Once we have used up the earth's supply of fossil fuels, they will be gone forever – they are nonrenewable sources of energy. We cannot wait millions of years for the next supply of fossil fuel to be formed, so we have to look for other ways of providing energy for people on the planet. We need to find renewable sources of energy – energy that can be used again and again. One source of renewable energy is plants.

▲ Plants convert and store energy from the sun by making starches and sugar – the process of photosynthesis. This stored energy can be made into a fuel that we can use. In Brazil and other countries, sugarcane (shown above) is grown to make alcohol. Once the cane has been cut down, its juice can be used to make a kind of alcohol called gasohol, as grape juice is made into wine. New cars that run on gasohol instead of gasoline have been designed.

◄ In some countries, including the United States and France, alcohol from plants is being added to ordinary gasoline to be used in cars.

Another way of using ▶ plants for energy is to mix the remains of plants, such as straw, with animal manure. Inside special containers called digesters, the animal and plant remains rot and make natural gas. This natural gas, called methane, is an excellent but rather smelly fuel. You can sometimes smell methane when you stir the mud in a pond or when someone passes wind. Methane can be burned to heat houses, generate electricity, and cook food. In countries with a lot of straw and a lot of animals, it could be a useful source of energy.

One of the problems of using plants to produce energy is that plants need a lot of land to grow on. The same land may be needed to produce food. A solution may be to grow plants that live under water. One plant tried in the United States is the water hyacinth, but it has grown so quickly that it is clogging rivers and lakes. It's difficult to find the perfect answer when it comes to energy!

Design a plant-powered machine
Make your own design for a machine that is powered by plant energy. Make a drawing of it and show on the drawing how it works. What sort of plants ◀ would you use?

ENERGY FROM WIND AND WATER

People need to make good use of renewable sources of energy. The sun is our most obvious direct supply, but other sources that we will need to use more and more in the future are wind, waves, and tides.

▲ At one time, many windmills were constructed to pump water and generate electricity. But, with the increased use of other more efficient sources of energy, such as coal and later oil, windmill use decreased. Since the 1970's, however, there has been renewed interest in the use of wind turbines (the modern name for windmills) as people become more aware of the need to find alternative sources of energy.

Wind turbines are used to generate electricity – some can make enough electricity to light 20,000 light bulbs at once! The problem is that they can make electricity only when the wind blows.

The waves on the sea ▶ possess tremendous energy as they crash into the coasts. We are still waiting for someone to think of a way of capturing the energy of the waves. One suggestion has been to use floats that bob up and down on the waves. The up-and-down motion of the floats could be used to make electricity. These bobbing floats have been called Salter's ducks, after their inventor.

The problem is that these floats would need to stretch out for hundreds of miles near coasts and harbors. They could be dangerous for ships and they could affect wildlife.

◀ The tides of the sea go in and out every day as a result of the pull of the moon's gravity. As the sea flows in and out, the movement of water can be used to drive turbines (as waterwheels do) which then generate electricity. In 1966, a tidal power plant for making electricity was built in Brittany, France. It can make enough electricity to provide heat and light for thousands of homes.

There are many other places where the energy of the tides could be harnessed, such as the Bristol Channel in England and along the coasts of Maine and Nova Scotia in North America. But, as with the waves, we need to be careful not to upset animal life when we are attempting to use the sea's energy.

SAVING PRECIOUS ENERGY

Energy is so precious that we cannot ▶ afford to waste it. This is more true than ever of fossil fuels. Yet, we are all very wasteful with energy. This photo shows a coal-fired power plant. A lot of the energy from the burning coal ends up going out of the big towers. For every house that could be heated by the electricity from this plant, another could be heated by the energy escaping as steam from the cooling towers. We need to find less wasteful ways of using our fossil fuel.

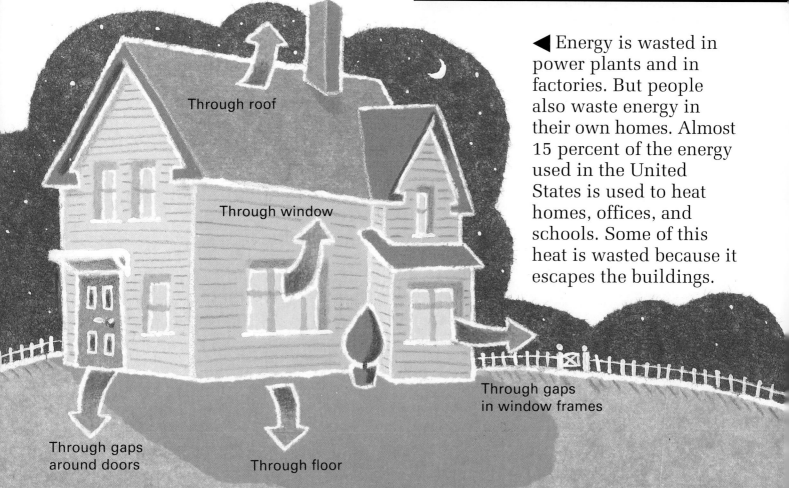

Through roof

Through window

◀ Energy is wasted in power plants and in factories. But people also waste energy in their own homes. Almost 15 percent of the energy used in the United States is used to heat homes, offices, and schools. Some of this heat is wasted because it escapes the buildings.

Through gaps in window frames

Through gaps around doors

Through floor

Energy can be saved by:
- Insulating attics and walls of a building.
- Putting a thick layer of insulating padding or blankets around hot water tanks to keep heat in.
- Putting weather stripping around doors and windows.
- Using storm windows.

This chart shows ▶ approximately how much energy (in kilocalories) could be saved each year in the average home.

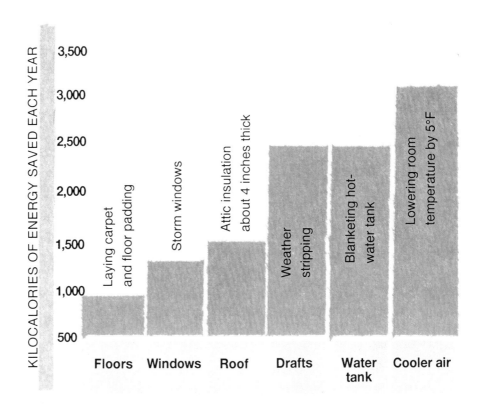

What can *you* do to save energy? There are lots of things that each one of us can do to help.
- Check that your home is well insulated.
- Turn off unneeded lights, especially if a room is empty.
- Many rooms in schools and homes are kept too warm. Ask if the thermostat can be turned down or a radiator switched off.
- Don't leave hot water faucets running or dripping.
- Insulate yourself – keep your body heat in!
- Don't overfill teakettles. Put in just the amount of water you need.

If everyone did these things, a massive amount of energy would be saved.

How can you save energy?

What other ideas can you think of for saving energy? Take a good look around at home and at school to see where energy is being wasted. What can you do to help save it?

ENERGY CONVERSION

There are many different kinds or forms of energy. All the time, energy is being changed from one of these forms to another. Electrical energy from the battery in a flashlight is changed to light and heat energy. This saxophonist changes chemical energy ◄ from his body into sound energy.

We only really notice energy when it is being changed, or converted, from one form into another. Two important energy converters on earth are plants and human beings. Plants convert energy from the sun into chemical energy in the form of sugar and starch. When human beings eat plants they are taking in this chemical energy. Then they can use it for walking, running, keeping warm, and growing. ▼

Sun's energy

Chemical energy

Doing work, moving around keeping warm, growing

In the last hundred years or so we have used more and more engines and machines to do our energy conversion (our work). This is one of the reasons why we are running out of fuel. A steam engine uses coal: the stored energy in the coal is converted into heat, which makes steam to drive the engine. Automobile engines convert the energy in gasoline into movement energy. Jet engines and rockets do the same thing. Nowadays, almost all of our energy converters are engines that use fuel. Once the energy in fuel has been converted into movement energy, we cannot get it back again. It ends up as heat that just goes into the air.

WOW! A rocket engine for a spacecraft can produce as much power as 500,000 car engines – but only for a short time.

Make a wind-up energy converter

You can make a vehicle that converts energy but does not need any fuel. All you need is an empty thread spool, a bead, three used wooden matches, and a small rubber band.

Put the rubber band through the bead and slip a match through it. Now pull the other end through the spool and hold it tight with half a match.

Place another match against this half by pushing it into one of the channels in the spool.

Now wind the vehicle up by turning the match in the bead. See how far you can get the vehicle to go. What kinds of energy are involved here? Where did the vehicle's energy come from in the first place?

23

WHEELS KEEP TURNING

In the United States, nearly one third of our energy is used to move people and goods from one place to another. Nearly all our transportation relies on engines. Cars, buses, trucks, trains, ships, and planes all have engines that need fuel. One day these fuels will run out – this is the energy problem with transportation.

Many people use automobiles to get ▶ around. Because of this, many cities are getting clogged with cars. In major cities, the average speed at which a car travels in moderate to heavy traffic is no faster than a horse and cart were able to travel in the city 100 years ago! In many city centers, people could get around just as quickly by bicycle.

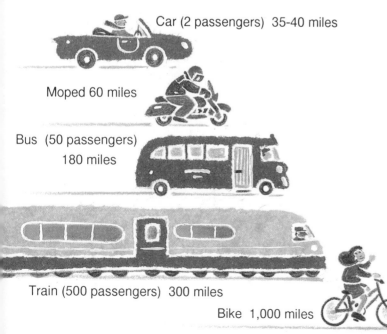

Car (2 passengers) 35-40 miles

Moped 60 miles

Bus (50 passengers) 180 miles

Train (500 passengers) 300 miles

Bike 1,000 miles

◀ Some kinds of transportation are much less energy hungry than others. This chart shows how many miles passengers can travel when different types of transportation use the same amount of energy. Private cars use a lot of energy. Travel by car, especially with only one or two passengers, wastes more energy than public transportation by train or bus. However, public transportation can be less convenient and reliable than travel by car.

Getting around by bicycle is best. ▶
Bicycles don't use fuel, but the cyclist
uses energy from food. Even with
helmets, however, bicycling in traffic
is much more dangerous than travel by
car or bus. With well marked cycling-
only lanes in cities and towns, cycling
would be much safer. Perhaps more
people would travel short distances by
bike and energy would be saved.

▲ In the future we will need to look
for different kinds of transportation, or
vehicles that use alternative sources of
energy. One idea that is being worked
on is the solar car. This has large solar
cells on its roof to capture the sun's
energy. This solar power is converted
into electricity, which is used to run
the engine. The only problem is, what
happens when the sun isn't shining?
One solution is to use large batteries
that store energy when the sun is
shining and keep the car going when
it is cloudy or dark.

ENERGY AROUND THE WORLD

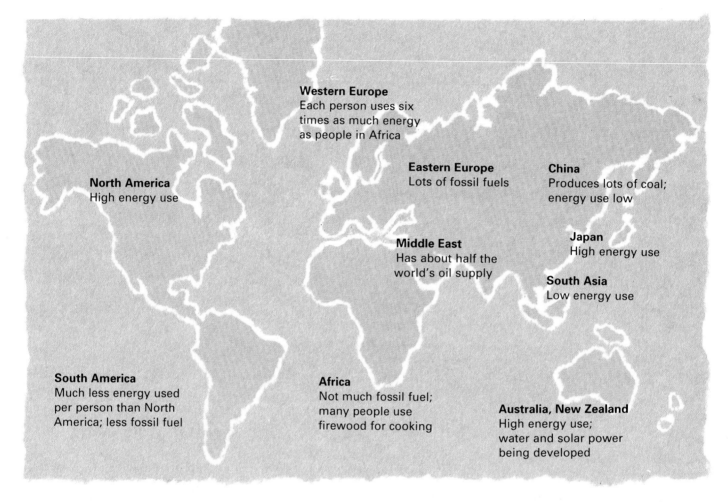

Western Europe
Each person uses six times as much energy as people in Africa

North America
High energy use

Eastern Europe
Lots of fossil fuels

China
Produces lots of coal; energy use low

Japan
High energy use

Middle East
Has about half the world's oil supply

South Asia
Low energy use

South America
Much less energy used per person than North America; less fossil fuel

Africa
Not much fossil fuel; many people use firewood for cooking

Australia, New Zealand
High energy use; water and solar power being developed

▲ One of the problems with the world's energy supply is that people in some countries use far more energy than people in other countries. A person living in North America uses seventeen times as much energy as someone living in southern Asia. In North America, people use energy to wash clothes and dishes, run cars, heat their houses (or keep them cool), mow the lawn, farm their food, and run factories. In countries in southern Asia, such as India and Malaysia, energy is used mostly for cooking food.

This chart shows how the electricity consumed in different continents compares with the size of the population. ▼

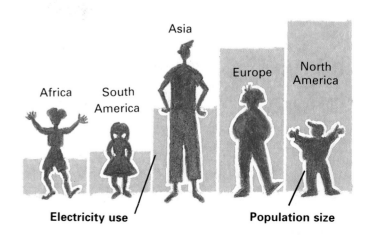

Africa

South America

Asia

Europe

North America

Electricity use

Population size

The same is true for the food eaten each day by people around the world. On average, people in the United States and Canada take in about twice as much food energy per day as people in India. ▼

| India 2,000 kcal | China 2,200 kcal | Japan 2,400 kcal | Great Britain 2,900 kcal | France 3,100 kcal | United States 3,200 kcal |

Many people in the energy hungry countries are very wasteful. They live in societies where many products are disposed of after they have been used. A lot of the packaging of goods sold in stores and supermarkets is very wasteful of energy and resources such as paper. Also, many of the goods used by people in these countries are not built to last for a long time. ▶

Goods that are made to last a short time before they are thrown away are wasteful of energy. Recycling things like bottles, jars, and cans does help, but even then, energy is needed to make the glass or metal into new containers. Using containers again and again, as we once did with milk bottles, is the best way of saving energy and resources.

ENERGY CRISIS?

The fuels we currently use – coal, oil, and natural gas – make other substances when they are burned. One of these substances is carbon dioxide. This is a gas that is already in the air. Carbon dioxide and some other gases in the air trap some of the sun's heat in the earth's atmosphere. These gases act like the glass of a greenhouse, keeping the air temperature inside warmer than outside. So these gases are called "greenhouse gases," and they create the greenhouse effect in the earth's atmosphere.

Some scientists believe that if there is too much carbon dioxide in our atmosphere a gradual warming of the earth will result. This could seriously affect our planet. Some people believe it could begin to melt ice caps in the North and South Poles, which could cause sea levels to rise. This would flood low-lying land near the sea. Global warming could also cause serious droughts in other places. This would prevent crops from growing, leading to famine and starvation. What can be done to avoid global warming?

The burning of all fossil fuels produces a lot of carbon dioxide, so we need to burn less of it. We have used fuels, mostly firewood, throughout history. Now we are living in the age of fossil fuels, but some of these could be used up by the end of the 21st century. ▶

We need to look for new ways of saving energy and for energy sources to replace the ones we use now. Wind, wave, solar, and nuclear energy might be used much more widely in the future. We must find energy sources that don't damage the planet and that all countries can share. It's not an easy problem to solve, but it's one of the most important problems that people face.

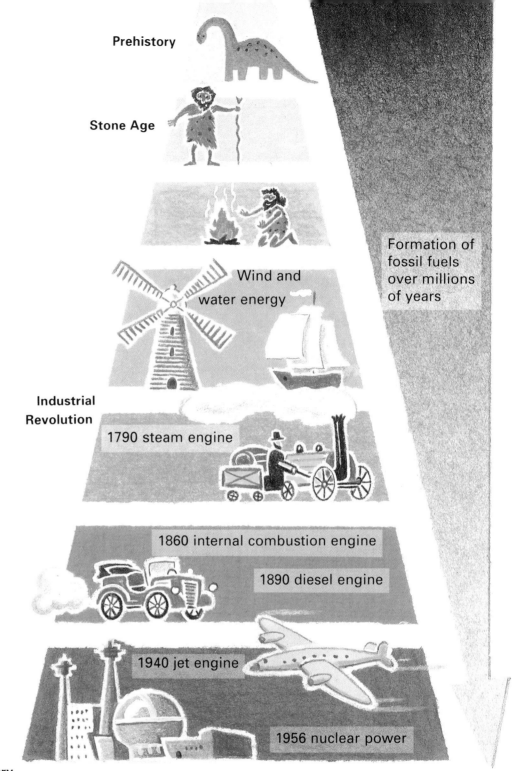

Prehistory

Stone Age

Formation of fossil fuels over millions of years

Wind and water energy

Industrial Revolution

1790 steam engine

1860 internal combustion engine

1890 diesel engine

1940 jet engine

1956 nuclear power

21st Century

Solar-powered transport and homes

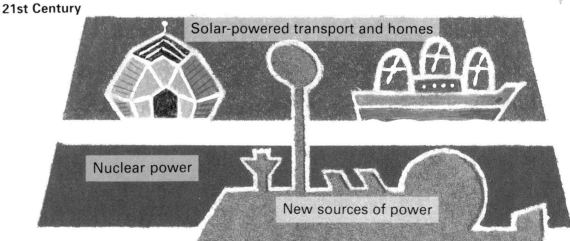

Nuclear power

New sources of power

GLOSSARY

Atmosphere   The layer of gases that surrounds the earth.

Calorie (cal)   The unit used in the United States to measure energy (heat). Since the calorie is so small, most measurements are given in kilocalories (kcal or Cal), or thousands of calories. (Kilocalories are often referred to as calories, as in food labels.)

Chemical energy   The energy stored in fuels or other chemicals that can be released, for example, through burning.

Droughts   Long periods without rain.

Energy converter   Anything that changes energy from one form to another – for example, a plant, an animal, or a machine.

Fossil fuel   A fuel formed a long time ago from the remains of dead plants or animals – for example, coal and oil.

Global warming   The threat of a gradual warming of the earth's atmosphere, which, some scientists believe, could take place if the greenhouse effect increases.

Greenhouse effect   The trapping of the sun's heat in the earth's atmosphere through the buildup of gases such as carbon dioxide.

Industry   The organized production of goods.

Nonrenewable sources of energy   Energy resources that, once they have been used up, cannot be replaced.

Photosynthesis   The process by which plants use sunlight to convert carbon dioxide and water to energy, in the form of sugars and starch, which is stored in the plant.

Renewable sources of energy   Energy resources that can be used again and again – for example, wind and tides.

Solar cells   Special cells that convert solar energy into electricity.

Solar energy   Energy in rays from the sun.

Thermostat   A device that is used to keep the temperature in a room at a constant level.

Wind turbine   A large modern structure, like a windmill, that converts the wind's energy into electricity.

BOOKS TO READ

Averous, Pierre. *The Atom.* Focus on Science. Chicago: Childrens Press, 1988.

Bailey, Donna. *Energy All Around Us.* Facts About. Milwaukee: Raintree Steck-Vaughn, 1990.

Bailey, Donna. *Energy from Oil and Gas.* Facts About. Milwaukee: Raintree Steck-Vaughn, 1990.

Bailey, Donna. *Energy for Our Bodies.* Facts About. Milwaukee: Raintree Steck-Vaughn, 1990.

Catherall, Ed. *Exploring Uses of Energy.* Exploring Science. Milwaukee: Raintree Steck-Vaughn, 1990.

Dunn, Andrew. *It's Electric.* How Things Work. New York: Thomson Learning, 1993.

Friedhoffer, Robert. *Forces, Motion, and Energy.* Scientific Magic. New York: Franklin Watts, 1992.

Jennings, Terry. *Energy.* The Young Scientist Investigates. Chicago: Childrens Press, 1989.

Hare, Tony. *The Greenhouse Effect.* Save Our Earth. New York: Gloucester Press, 1990.

Harlow, Rosie and Morgan, Gareth. *Energy and Growth.* Fun With Science. New York: Warwick Press, 1991.

Keeler, Barbara. *Energy Alternatives.* Lucent Books, 1990.

Kerrod, Robin. *Energy Resources.* World's Resources. New York: Thomson Learning, 1994.

McKie, Robin. *Energy.* Science Frontiers. New York: Hampstead Press, 1989.

Rickard, Graham. *Oil.* Resources. Thomson Learning, 1993.

Rickard, Graham. *Water Energy.* Milwaukee: Gareth Stevens, Inc., 1991.

Rickard, Graham. *Wind Energy.* Milwaukee: Gareth Stevens, Inc., 1991.

Taylor, Barbara. *Energy and Power.* Science Starters. Franklin Watts, 1990.

INDEX